EVEN NUMBERS

By CHARLES GHIGNA

Illustrations by MISA SABURI

Music by ERIK KOSKINEN

CANTATA
LEARNING

WWW.CANTATALEARNING.COM

CANTATA
LEARNING

Published by Cantata Learning
1710 Roe Crest Drive
North Mankato, MN 56003
www.cantatalearning.com

Library of Congress Cataloging-in-Publication Data
Names: Ghigna, Charles. | Saburi, Misa, illustrator. | Koskinen, Erik.
Title: Even numbers / by Charles Ghigna ; illustrations by Misa Saburi ;
  music by Erik Koskinen.
Description: North Mankato, MN : Cantata Learning, [2018] | Series: Winter
  math | Audience: Age 3-8. | Audience: K to grade 3.
Identifiers: LCCN 2017007565 (print) | LCCN 2017017635 (ebook) | ISBN
  9781684100248 | ISBN 9781684100231 (hardcover : alk. paper)
Subjects: LCSH: Numbers, Natural--Juvenile literature. | Counting--Juvenile
  literature.
Classification: LCC QA141.3 (ebook) | LCC QA141.3 .G4794 2018 (print) | DDC
  512.7/2--dc23
LC record available at https://lccn.loc.gov/2017007565

Book design, Tim Palin Creative
Editorial direction, Flat Sole Studio
Executive musical production and direction, Elizabeth Draper
Music arranged and produced by Erik Koskinen

Printed in the United States of America in North Mankato, Minnesota.
072017   0367CGF17

ACCESS THE MUSIC!

SCAN CODE WITH MOBILE APP

CANTATALEARNING.COM

TIPS TO SUPPORT LITERACY AT HOME

WHY READING AND SINGING WITH YOUR CHILD IS SO IMPORTANT

Daily reading with your child leads to increased academic achievement. Music and songs, specifically rhyming songs, are a fun and easy way to build early literacy and language development. Music skills correlate significantly with both phonological awareness and reading development. Singing helps build vocabulary and speech development. And reading and appreciating music together is a wonderful way to strengthen your relationship.

READ AND SING EVERY DAY!

TIPS FOR USING CANTATA LEARNING BOOKS AND SONGS DURING YOUR DAILY STORY TIME

1. As you sing and read, point out the different words on the page that rhyme. Suggest other words that rhyme.

2. Memorize simple rhymes such as Itsy Bitsy Spider and sing them together. This encourages comprehension skills and early literacy skills.

3. Use the questions in the back of each book to guide your singing and storytelling.

4. Read the included sheet music with your child while you listen to the song. How do the music notes correlate to the words of the song?

5. Sing along on the go and at home. Access music by scanning the QR code on each Cantata book. You can also stream or download the music for free to your computer, smartphone, or mobile device.

Devoting time to daily reading shows that you are available for your child. Together, you are building language, literacy, and listening skills.

Have fun reading and singing!

Every number is either even or odd. How do you tell the difference? The children in the story see many wonderful things during the winter season. They have learned that if they can pair these things up into groups of two, then they have an even number.

Turn the page to learn how to tell if a number is even. Remember to sing along!

Look here and over there,
even numbers are everywhere.

Look here and over there,
even numbers come in pairs.

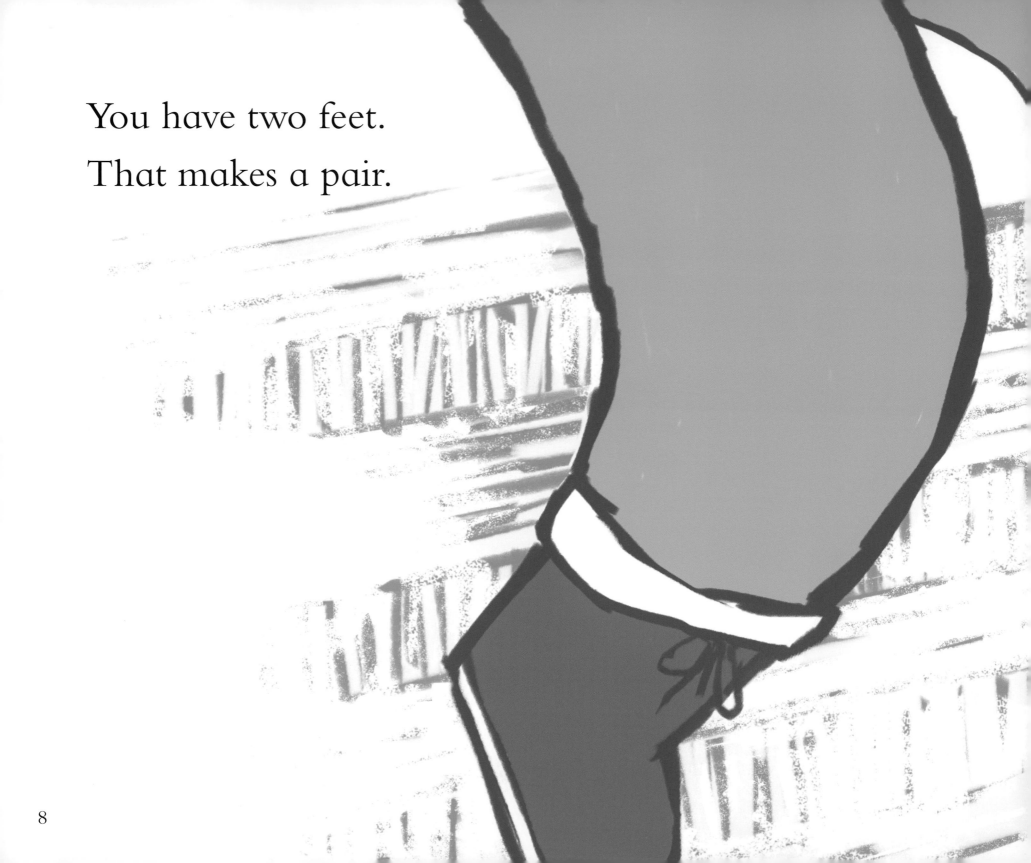

You have two feet.
That makes a pair.

Two feet stomping,
stomping down the stairs.

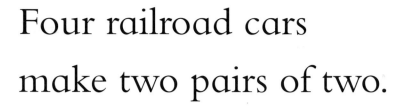

Four railroad cars
make two pairs of two.

Around the track,
they chugga choo!

Six **blinking** lights
make three pairs of two.

They light up the night
in green, yellow, and blue!

Eight marshmallows
make four pairs of two.

In hot cocoa,
they melt into **goo**!

Ten **icicles**
make five pairs of two.

They hang from the roof,
dripping splish, splash, sploosh!

Let's get these even numbers straight.
If it ends in 0, 2, 4, 6, or 8, it is even.

35

40

16

27

55

93

26

52

12

98

34

83

100

76

68

20

Now use this helpful clue
to find the even numbers in front you.

Look here and over there,
even numbers are everywhere.

Look here and over there,
even numbers come in pairs.

SONG LYRICS
Even Numbers

Look here and over there,
even numbers are everywhere.
Look here and over there,
even numbers come in pairs.

You have two feet.
That makes a pair.
Two feet stomping,
stomping down the stairs.

Four railroad cars
make two pairs of two.
Around the track,
they chugga choo-hoo!

Six blinking lights
make three pairs of two.
They light up the night
in green, yellow, and blue!

Eight marshmallows
make four pairs of two.
In hot cocoa,
they melt into goo!

Ten icicles
make five pairs of two.
They hang from the roof,
dripping splish, splash, sploosh!

Let's get these even numbers straight.
If it ends 0, 2, 4, 6, or 8, it is even.
Now use this helpful clue
to find the even numbers in front you.

Look here and over there,
even numbers are everywhere.

Look here and over there,
even numbers come in pairs.

Even Numbers

Americana (with a New Orleans Feel)
Erik Koskinen

Verse 2
Four railroad cars
make two pairs of two.
Around the track,
they chugga choo-hoo!

Verse 3
Six blinking lights
make three pairs of two.
They light up the night
in green, yellow, and blue!

Verse 4
Eight marshmallows
make four pairs of two.
In hot cocoa,
they melt into goo!

Verse 5
Ten icicles
make five pairs of two.
They hang from the roof,
dripping splish, splash, sploosh!

GLOSSARY

blinking—when lights go on and off

goo—a sticky substance

icicles—hanging pieces of ice that formed by water dripping and freezing

GUIDED READING ACTIVITIES

1. What is winter like where you live? What things do you see in winter? Are some of them mentioned in this song?

2. This song mentions a clue to know whether a number is even. Remember what it is? Look back on pages 18 and 19. Then write down as many even numbers as you can think of.

3. Listen to this song again. When you here a number sung, clap your hands that many times. So when you hear the number "two," clap your hands twice.

TO LEARN MORE

Clay, Kathryn. *All About Winter Weather*. North Mankato, MN: Capstone, 2016.

Deen, Marilyn. *Odd and Even*. North Mankato, MN: Capstone, 2013.

DeGezelle, Terri. *Exploring Winter*. North Mankato, MN: Capstone: 2012.

Ghinga, Charles, *Odd Numbers*. North Mankato, MN: Cantata Learning, 2018.